For Irene Nichols
from the
cutter of wood.
Michael McCurdy
2 MAR 83

Wood Engravings by Michael McCurdy

TOWARD
THE LIGHT

The Porcupine's Quill, Erin

Published by the Porcupine's Quill, Inc., 68 Main Street, Erin, Ontario, Canada NOB 1TO. Distributed by Firefly Books, 3520 Pharmacy Avenue, Unit 1C, Scarborough, Ontario, Canada M1W 2T8.

Several of these engravings may also be purchased as original artist's prints by writing Michael McCurdy at R.D. 2, Box 145, Great Barrington, Massachusetts, U.S.A. 01230.

Typeset in Palatino by Howarth & Smith Limited (Toronto). Printed and bound by the Porcupine's Quill, in November of 1982, on Zephyr Antique Laid.

The frontispiece, *Unfinished Hopkins, Dublin*, is from *Gerard Manley Hopkins Meets Walt Whitman in Heaven and Other Poems* — Penmaen Press's twenty-first publication — a series of poems about the Jesuit poet Hopkins, written by Philip Dacey. It was Hopkins' poem 'Penmaen Pool' which provided the source for McCurdy's imprint *Penmaen Press*.

Cover illustration is entitled *The Binder's Curse*, 1981.

ISBN 0-88984-062-8

Introduction

The prints shown in this book represent some eighteen years of attempting to push back masses of black and cut outward toward the light. With engraving tools called burins, the wood block must be carefully shaved away to reveal what will appear as white in the finished print. I am reminded of the feeling Michelangelo is said to have had as he chipped away at a block of stone, a sense that he was setting free the captive figure inside.

Early on, that awful blackness seemingly overran the light, as in some of the early prints shown in this book. But my original presentation of form in white lines and stippled dots has given way to a recent preference for a more balanced play of white and black line coupled with a variety of textures and tonalities.

Unlike the woodcut, the wood engraving is a fairly modern technique, developed in the late eighteenth century by Thomas Bewick, among others. Throughout the nineteenth century, the engraving was increasingly relegated to the status of a means of commercial reproduction. It was used to reproduce the pictures that were increasingly in demand for such periodicals as *Harper's Weekly* and *Frank Leslie's Illustrated Newspaper*. The wood block was drawn upon by the artist, while gangs of skillful engravers did the actual cutting of the design, sometimes breaking up the block so that each could work independently on a single section of the wood block. In time, other methods of reproduction — the half-tone engraving and the photographic linecut — displaced thousands of engravers, and the wood engraving — that 'fine art of scratch' as Ruskin called it — appeared moribund. A renewed use of the wood engraving as an art form in itself began in the early part of this century, as artists returned to the cutting of blocks and the technique gained increased acceptance as a valid graphic art.

The wood blocks used for the prints in this book are either boxwood or maple. Most are the former. Boxwood is a slow-growing tree and quite hard. The log is sliced, as one might slice a banana, whereupon the best sections of each slice are stored and aged for several years. Then the separate little pieces are glued together and formed into type-high blocks, highly polished, and are able to be locked into a printing form in the same way as metal type. With engraving, the cutting is done on the end grain in contrast to the woodcut in which work is done on the side grain, giving the woodcut its rough-hewn appearance and grainy texture.

The engraving isn't for everyone. Artists today generally prefer a larger canvas on which to display their emotional reactions to the world. Many printmakers go in for large prints, filled with color, sometimes competing, it would seem, with painters. Big effects, splashy effects. Somehow the contemplative quiet that one may associate with the wood engraving seems out of tune with the intensity of our age. But as with all art, it depends on the vision and the skill of the artist whether the work sings or doesn't sing.

The wood engraving is an honest medium. It's straightforward, and there is no room for error. No room for cover-up. A cut is made, and it stays. I don't know a single contemporary engraver who goes to the bother of repairing a bad block by drilling away the error and inserting a plug to engrave over again. And I've always had a feeling that this is another reason wood engraving is not enormously popular as a technique among artists. It can't hide one's weaker moments.

The engravings in this book are quite small. This is largely because nearly all of them were intended for books. Most were not engraved for their own sake, even though they may stand alone. Their fundamental reason for being was to accompany a text. This is why I have always called myself a 'book artist'. For years, I have married my visual work with the printed word. A number of the blocks here were cut for my own *Penmaen Press* publications — books of contemporary fiction, poetry and translation. And the radical difference in the texts which I have illustrated accounts for their wide range of style.

So one could say that most of the engravings shown here are illustrative in nature. It could be argued that all art is illustrative, or should be. And although they strike me as individual, I am ever mindful that they relate to something beyond my own peculiar compulsion to express particular ideas and feelings.

The circumstances surrounding the cutting of these blocks are as much a part of this book as the engravings themselves. I have written brief anecdotes for most of them, as they all have a story, and seeing them stretched out in this manner makes for a kind of personal history. And although I trust the engravings speak for themselves, it has been a pleasure for me to speak along with them!

Whenever I was certain as to the month an engraving was begun, I included it along with the year. This date indicates only when the engraving was begun in the cutting stages. Often, engravings would take many months

— worked on intermittently. Only two engravings were completed in record time: *Robert Frost* (number 32), which was finished in one morning, and *Clear Sky* (number 34), which was completed in one day.

Michael McCurdy
Great Barrington,
Massachusetts

There are no authentic likenesses of the founder of the Religious Society of Friends, the Quakers. But I felt the need to try my hand at a portrait, which was used on the prospectus for my first Penmaen Press book, *The Quaker Queries,* issued in 1969. Not included in the book itself, the engraving was printed separately and slipped in.

It must have been the ancient ruins that conjured up this fantasy, for my wife and I were in Rome during October when this block was begun. There is more black line and open white here, reminiscent of work that I knew by Leonard Baskin and George Lockwood.

On our return from Europe, I started working at a graphics studio in Boston. Before that I had planned on printing Whitman's great poem 'Song of the Open Road', for which I had cut this block. The graphics studio took up the Whitman project, but it was dropped for economic reasons.

I began my work as a free-lance book illustrator and designer, and the fledgling printer and publisher David R. Godine commissioned me to design and illustrate *The Journal of Madam Knight*. During this time, I was asked to do an engraving of the small barn where Godine and his young crew printed their books, on the grounds of the American Academy of Arts and Sciences in Brookline. It was like a piece of Vermont, and only a stone's throw from Boston. It also marked the beginning of Godine's career.

Written in 1704 by Sarah Kemble Knight, who lived from 1666 to 1727, *The Journal of Madam Knight* is a fascinating and earthy account of her travels on horseback from Boston to New York. It was first published in 1825. I cut six engravings for the journal, four of which are pictured on the following pages.

7 Old New York, 1971

8 *Madam Knight Views a Sheep*, 1971

While *Madam Knight* was in press, I was working on the idea of doing Arthur Ransome's translation of the Russian folk tale, *A Soldier and Death*, from a little book that had belonged to my great-grandmother. I cut this block and made some preliminary drawings for other engravings but, for economic reasons again, the book never materialized.

I cut this little portrait of the young Benjamin Franklin at the request of the Society of Printers, to which I had just been elected. It appeared as a keepsake for Boston's Printing and Publishing Week.

In the grand old tradition of the Limited Editions Club, the Imprint Society of Barre, Massachusetts produced a long list of finely wrought books. Among them was *The Journal of Alvar Nuñez Cabeza de Vaca*, designed and printed by Roderick Stinehour. I cut a number of engravings of which six appear here.

13 *Parrot*, 1971

14 *Indian Huts, 1972*

15 *Fish and Fruit,* MARCH 1972

16 *Indian, 1972*

When my own Penmaen Press was searching for its second book, I turned to the work of my poet-friend William Ferguson. He came up with six haiku-like poems, and I cut a small engraving to accompany each. The following two cuts were rejects, as I felt they weren't right for the book. But I include them here on their own merits.

The next engraving was used on the title page in Penmaen Press's third book *Dove at the Windows*. Four Quakers were hanged on the Boston Common in the seventeenth century, and all of them wrote expressive and courageous letters from their jail cells just before their execution. The title of the book was taken from William Leddra's 'I am a dove at the windows of the ark'. I hand-set these letters and printed the limited edition by hand.

Early in 1974, my physician-scholar friend George E. Gifford, Jr. approached me about doing the engravings for his next book, *Cecil County, Maryland, 1608-1850*, which he planned to have privately printed. Nineteen engravings resulted, four of which are reproduced here.

21 *George Whitefield, Preaching,* MAY 1974

22 *Roger's Tavern, Charlestown,* MAY 1974

23 *Canvasback Duck,* JUNE 1974

The Boston publisher David Godine was issuing a series of first edition poetry chapbooks, and the only one to use art was X.J. Kennedy's book of poems. In fact, the poet himself asked me to cut this title-page engraving, which sought to convey the ludicrous idea found in the title poem.

X.J. Kennedy and I continued our relationship in print by collaborating on my press's fourth book, *Celebrations After the Death of John Brennan*, an elegy for a student of his who had committed suicide. The book was hand-printed in a limited edition of 300 copies and included the three engravings shown here. All were cut between August and October, 1974.

26 *Gowned As a Clown*, 1974

These three tiny initial engravings were commissioned by the *Atlantic Monthly* for a story by the late William Saroyan. This opportunity opened up communication between the writer and myself and resulted in my publishing two of his original stories with Helen Siegl as the illustrator.

Penmaen's fifth book was a selection of impressionistic poems by the New York poet and photographer Gerard Malanga, and this engraving, printed in gray, was used on the title page. In it I sought to incorporate the variety of images found throughout the book.

I had been visiting the poet Richard Eberhart in Hanover, New Hampshire. While relaxing in his living room, we came up with the idea of a collaboration. Dick had a series of poems about poets he had known either personally or vicariously. It was decided. We would print and publish these, and I would cut an engraved portrait to accompany each poem. The result was *Poems to Poets*, published in 1976. A selection from that work follows.

31 *Wallace Stevens, 1975*

Richard Eberhart led me on to other book projects with Allen Ginsberg and Leo Connellan. My contact with Connellan resulted in the publication of *Crossing America*, a tough, hard-hitting narrative of the poet's life on the skids during the 1950's. The scene shown here, used on the book's title page, astounded the poet by its resemblance to the view he remembered from his room on Eddy Street in San Francisco.

My actor friend, Christopher Childs, compiled passages from many Thoreau sources for his successful stage monologue *Clear Sky, Pure Light: an Evening with Henry David Thoreau*. We decided to transcribe it into book form, using the same title. The engraving shown here is from that book.

King Harald and the Icelanders, Penmaen Press's twelfth book, was translated from the Icelandic by my friend Pardee Lowe, Jr. I approached these nine-hundred-year-old stories in a purely illustrative fashion, seeking to capture the primitive flavor of the stark narrative.

This engraving was commissioned by the *Atlantic Monthly* for a story entitled 'Winter Oak', which appeared in the September, 1979 issue of the magazine. The composition and general approach here is a tribute to Lynd Ward, a fine wood engraver who greatly influenced my direction.

The following two engravings are from Osmond Beckwith's *Vernon*, cut for the publisher, Breaking Point.

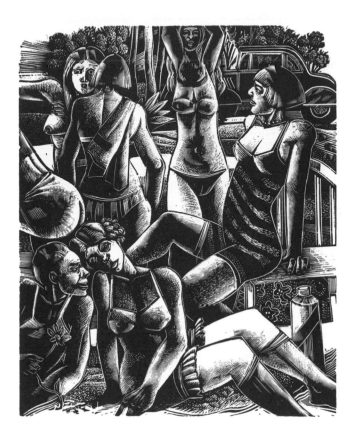

The next six engravings shown here are from the Bieler Press book *Everything That Has Been Shall Be Again: Reincarnation Fables by John Gilgun*. Issued in a small, hand-printed letterpress edition from St. Paul, Minnesota, as well as in an offset paperback, a print is featured at the beginning of each of the nine fables.

43 *Ant*, 1980

44 *Cow*, 1980

45 Hen, 1980

46 Bear, 1980

47 *Peacock*, 1980

This served as the title page engraving for *Elizabeth*, a story by Brian Swann in Penmaen Press's series of novellas. It's a touching story of a Russian émigrée growing old in America, surrounded by a household of cats and dogs, friends and spirits. I tried to capture that swirling madness around Elizabeth: the handyman to her right, ghosts from her aristocratic Russian background above her, she herself clutching the perennial cigarette.

A young Czech-American who had photographed the city of Prague wanted me to engrave a picture of the city for the title page of his photographic portfolio. The engraving shown on top was started in Florida, where my days were saturated with sunshine, but it would not do, for it looked too sunny and too Latin. A second engraving was requested and I was urged to make it as dismal and gray as I could. Prague was described to me as a gray city, a smoky city, so I had to hold down the white as much as possible. I even stripped the trees of their leaves in the bottom engraving, in an attempt to conjure up the bleakness that was called for.

This engraving was one of about nine cut for the University of Georgia Press for their book *Tygers of Wrath: Poems of Hate, Anger and Invective*, edited and compiled by X.J. Kennedy.

Another project for the University of Georgia Press, this is a frontispiece engraving for their book *Flannery O'Connor: The Imagination of Extremity.* The idea for the print came from the people at the Press, who wished to avoid using a peacock in association with Flannery O'Connor, a symbol apparently much overused in connection with the Georgia author. The incident shown takes place at the end of an O'Connor story called 'Greenleaf', and I believe we succeeded in achieving an effect quite opposite to that of a peacock!

My press's twentieth book was the first English edition of *World Alone* (*Mundo a Solas*) by the Nobel Prize-winning Spanish poet Vicente Aleixandre. These poems are no doubt the most pessimistic ones ever put into book form by the poet, and images of the moon and dark landscapes pervade the entire work. Incidentally, *Woman and Moon* (number 53) was destroyed while printing the book's jacket. A small piece of lead had somehow dropped onto the block and was crushed into the block's surface in the shape of a perfect rectangle.

53 *Woman and Moon,* 1981

Here are two illustrations for *The Lightning-rod Man* published by Daedalus Press in Minneapolis, Minnesota. In this obscure story by Herman Melville, the lightning-rod salesman seems harmless enough at first encounter, but grows increasingly menacing toward the end of the story.

55 *Lightning-rod Man, No. 2, 1981*

These next three engravings were commissioned by my old friend and associate Robert Hauser. Each was intended for a broadside concerned with some facet of the book arts, and two contain hilarious old poems unearthed by Hauser for this project. The first block shown here was cut in January, 1973, while the other two were done late in 1981 — an example of how long some projects just seem to take, or how fast time goes past.

MICHAEL MCCURDY was born in New York City in 1942. He is a graduate of the School of the Museum of Fine Arts in Boston, as well as Tufts University. McCurdy has designed and illustrated books for many publishers, both for the trade and the fine small press, in addition to publishing numerous titles himself under the imprint of *Penmaen Press*. He has had exhibitions of his books and engravings, and recent articles about the artist and his work have appeared in *North American Review, The Boston Phoenix, American Book Collector, The Malahat Review* (Victoria, B.C.) and *Art New England*. The well-known engraver and illustrator Fritz Eichenberg has written an article about McCurdy which appeared in the German magazine *Illustration 63*. Michael McCurdy lives in Great Barrington, Massachusetts, with his wife Deborah and their two children.